HAWAIIAN QUILTING

Instructions and Full-Size Patterns for 20 Blocks

by Elizabeth Root

Dover Publications, Inc. · New York

Additional designs are available from:

Hawaiian Designing Collection
P. O. Box 1396
Kailua, Hawaii 96734

Key to Cover Photographs

Front Cover

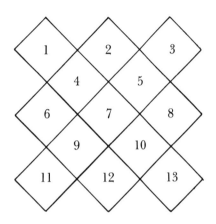

Back Cover

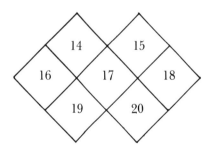

1. Maile, *page 29*
2. Hoya, *page 24*
3. Anthurium, *page 12*
4. Plumeria, *page 36*
5. Red Ginger, *page 40*
6. Hibiscus, *page 21*
7. Pineapple, *page 33*
8. Blue Jade, *page 13*
9. Crown Flower, *page 20*
10. Calla Lily, *page 17*
11. Breadfruit, *page 16*
12. Orchid, *page 32*
13. Angel's Trumpet, *page 9*
14. Iris, *page 25*
15. Kukui, *page 28*
16. Wood Rose, *page 48*
17. Water Lily, *page 45*
18. Tuberose, *page 44*
19. Protea, *page 37*
20. Trumpet Vine, *page 41*

Copyright © 1989 by Elizabeth Root.
All rights reserved under Pan American and International Copyright Conventions.

Published in Canada by General Publishing Company, Ltd., 30 Lesmill Road, Don Mills, Toronto, Ontario.
Published in the United Kingdom by Constable and Company, Ltd.

Hawaiian Quilting: Instructions and Full-Size Patterns for 20 Blocks is a new work, first published by Dover Publications, Inc., in 1989.

Manufactured in the United States of America
Dover Publications, Inc., 31 East 2nd Street, Mineola, N.Y. 11501

Library of Congress Cataloging-in-Publication Data

Root, Elizabeth.
    Hawaiian quilting : instructions and full-size patterns for 20 blocks / by Elizabeth Root.
        p.   cm. — (Dover needlework series)
    ISBN 0-486-25948-X
    1. Quilting—Hawaii—Patterns. I. Title. II. Series.
TT835.R66   1989
746.9'7041'09969—dc19   88-31782
                                                                              CIP

Introduction

A Hawaiian quilt, first seen, is rarely forgotten. Not only does it possess a strikingly beautiful pattern, but it has an unexplainable quality which originates more from the spirit of the design than from the stitches created by the quilter's hand.

Hawaiian quilting differs from that which evolved in other parts of the world. Its unique method of design, with its intricate quilting, has always been and continues to be more a form of artistic expression than a well-designed utilitarian necessity.

Hawaii's mild climate allowed this expression to be created in leisurely fashion, with far more time available for detailed appliqué and quilting than was possible in colder climes. The Hawaiians were not dependent upon the finishing of a quilt to ensure a warm night's rest during the winter months. This was fortunate, as a full-sized Hawaiian quilt, even for the experienced, takes about a year of continuous stitching to complete.

Four methods of constructing and designing a quilt, when combined, make the Hawaiian quilting process unique. These include the use of whole pieces of fabric for the appliqué and background; the "snowflake" method of cutting the design all at one time; the use of usually only two colors of fabric; and the echo, or outline, style of quilting, which follows the contour of the appliquéd design throughout the entire quilt.

The actual emergence of this quilting style is pure speculation, as, to date, no information has been found to substantiate any one theory. However, many things in the life-style of the "pre-missionary" Hawaiians helped to evolve the unique methods used in the Hawaiian quilt.

First, the Hawaiian women were already skilled in making bedding and everyday clothing from *tapa*,* a felted "fabric" made from the fibers of a native plant. The *tapa* was beaten, rather than cut, to the proper size for bedding and wraparound garments. The early whaling and trading ships brought the skills of sewing and the basic woven fabrics to the Hawaiians. They, in turn, created garments similar to the present-day *muumuu*. These were cut using the whole piece of fabric. There were no scraps left to be saved for the patchwork quilts of the style taught by the American missionaries upon their arrival in the early 1800s. As the cutting up of a large piece of fabric into little pieces which were then to be sewn back together again was illogical to the Hawaiian women, they soon created their own style of cutting the appliqué all at once from a whole piece of fabric.

Second, the "snowflake" art of paper cutting taught by the missionaries probably inspired the cutting method of the appliquéd designs the Hawaiian women used on their quilts. While they may have never related to the term "snowflake," the designs that resulted from the paper cutting resembled those used in the dye-stamped designs on their *tapas*. They quickly adopted the method, first folding their design fabric into eighths (or quarters) and then cutting the entire appliqué at one time, ensuring a balanced, symmetrical design.

Third, the use of usually only two colors—one for the design appliqué and a contrasting one for the background—probably arose from the initial unavailability of a selection of colored fabrics. Many of the early quilts were a combination of red and white, the two colors most commonly available. The practice of using dual colors prevailed, however, even after the selection of fabrics expanded. Occasionally a third or fourth color was used to accent a specific flower or part of the design. Sometimes two tones of the same color were used, or a small print and a solid color. But traditionally, throughout the years, the original concept of two contrasting colors has remained, accentuating the bold designs with striking clarity.

Fourth, the method of quilting turned from the geometric designs taught and practiced at the missionary schools, to the method of echo or outline quilting. The quilts first seen by the Hawaiians were, quite probably, the finest in the collections brought by the early missionaries. Many of these quilts may have contained examples of quilting techniques and patterns, such as echo quilting, that were far too intricate and time-consuming for the majority of quilts needed to ward off cold New England winters. While the Hawaiians, because of their own weaving abilities with native materials, were able to relate to the geometric patterns of traditional American quilting, the echo quilting appealed to their natural sense of grace and motion. The undulating lines following the contour of the appliquéd design looked like the waves and tides surrounding their islands. The Hawaiian women, being poetic and in touch with nature, adopted this quilting method, perhaps originally as being a *feeling* of Hawaii to be incorporated into their quilts rather than as merely a beautiful quilting technique. Feelings were very much a part of the designs of the Hawaiian quilt. The Hawaiians, born with a special relationship to the land and its products, and with a natural gracefulness, brought these qualities to the designs of their quilts.

The ability to create a beautiful, well-balanced design was considered a true gift and was a talent that was carefully guarded. Many believed that the spirit of the person creating and stitching the quilt became an

---

Tapa, the term in general use, is actually a Marquesan word; in the Hawaiian language, the word is *kapa*.

integral part of the finished work, giving it an added dimension—a sense of life. It has been suggested that, because of this belief, many of the earlier quilts made by the Hawaiian women had no openings in the central portion of the design. This was so that the part of their spirit that was considered a part of the quilt would not be able to wander. The belief also caused many quilts to be burned upon the death of their creators, thus allowing their spirits to pass on with them in their entirety.

The humid climate and salt air claimed many more of the early quilts. Of those remaining, many are stored away in family chests, carefully passed down from generation to generation, without being shown to people outside the immediate family. The art of making the Hawaiian quilt was considered so precious that it has only been in the last decade that the techniques have been openly shared. Now, in an attempt to perpetuate the art, its techniques are being taught, ensuring it its rightful place in the world of quilting, with full credit to the ingenuity and creativity of the Hawaiian people.

To give a quilt was indeed to give of one's self, and so quilts were only given to close relatives and friends. The design of each quilt was guarded, the work being done in the privacy of the quilter's home and not shown until the quilt was completed. Subtle songs were created and sung in public to chastise and embarrass an unauthorized "borrower" of a pattern. Designs were often drawn directly onto the folded fabric to be cut, thus eliminating patterns that could be copied. Authorized use of a design usually meant permission granted to a friend or relative to take her own pattern directly from the finished quilt. This inaccurate method of copying, the natural creativity that prompted spontaneous "improvements" and the use of different colors caused many patterns having the same name to look very different. As long as the basic outline of the original design was recognizable, the quilt kept the original name. It took a skilled designer to alter this outline and a brave one to then rename the pattern.

Names of quilts were often deceptive. Those using natural leaves or flowers, scenes, events or objects were easily defined, but because many quilts were the result of an emotional or highly personal event in the quilter's life, many of the patterns bore little or no resemblance to the names. In addition, the literal English translation of the Hawaiian name often changed the connotations of words, obscuring the sentiment. Sometimes the real meaning of a design that had great personal significance was known only to the designer. Giving an outsider a name for the design quite different from the real meaning allowed her to keep her true feelings a secret. Or, if the subject touched on the risqué, it was well hidden by double meanings and complicated translation.

Quilting also provided a way to record history. Many an event—the birth of a king, the finding of pearls in Hawaiian waters, the first gaslights in the royal palace—was put into a design and lovingly quilted by the Hawaiian women. Many of these quilts were then presented as gifts to the ruling monarch; some, fortunately, remain in collections today.

Probably the most revered pattern, which was designed and quilted in many ways, was "My Beloved Flag." With the overthrow of the monarchy in 1893, the Hawaiian flag was lowered. The Hawaiian people, fearing that they would never see their flag again, put its design, often combined with other symbols of royalty, into a pattern that was quilted and kept out of sight in many homes. The more daring made reversible quilts and canopies for their beds—on one side a traditional Hawaiian pattern and on the other, boldly quilted, their Hawaiian flag.

Hence, the development of Hawaiian quilting has been more than the amassing of a collection of strikingly beautiful designs. On the surface it has been the evolution of an entirely unique method of quilting. Underlying it is the embodiment of the spirit of a people rich in creativity and sensitivity, who, through this art form, shared not only their history and personal observations, but their feelings and sentiments during a time in their lives filled with extraordinary change and emotion.

General Instructions

This book contains instructions and full-size patterns for twenty different 18″-square Hawaiian quilt blocks. All of the designs are based on tropical flowers and plants found in the Hawaiian Islands.

MATERIALS

Fabric. 100% cotton percale is recommended because it is the easiest to work with, but any fabric of similar weight and weave may be used. Before cutting your fabric squares, wash all of the fabrics, let them dry, then press them thoroughly. For each quilt block, you will need to cut a 16″ square of fabric for the appliqué design and two 20″ squares of fabric for the background and backing (the extra 2″ will be taken up in the quilting). If you plan to make a pillow, you can use muslin for the backing since it will not be seen; otherwise, the backing should be the same type of fabric as the background. For a pillow, you will also need a 20″ square of fabric for the pillow back.

Batting. A 20″ square of bonded polyester batting. The thicker the batting you use, the more pronounced will be the contour of the quilting. 3.3-oz. to 5-oz. batting is recommended.

Thread. Cotton-wrapped polyester thread to match the appliqué and background. Thread made specifically for quilting is available, but regular sewing thread may be used.

Needles. No. 8 or No. 9 sharps for appliqué; No. 7 to No. 9 betweens for quilting.

Large quilting hoop.

Sharp scissors.

Straight pins.

Thimble.

Water-erasable marking pen (optional).

18″ pillow form (for pillow).

CUTTING AND BASTING THE DESIGN

Cut the pattern out of the book or trace it; cut the appliqué, background, batting and backing squares as specified under "Materials." Following *Figs. 1–4*, fold the appliqué and background squares into eighths; crease to mark the folds. Place the pattern on the folded appliqué square, matching the centers and fold lines (*Fig. 5*); pin securely. Cut out the design (*Fig. 6*); do not cut along the fold lines. Unfold the design and the

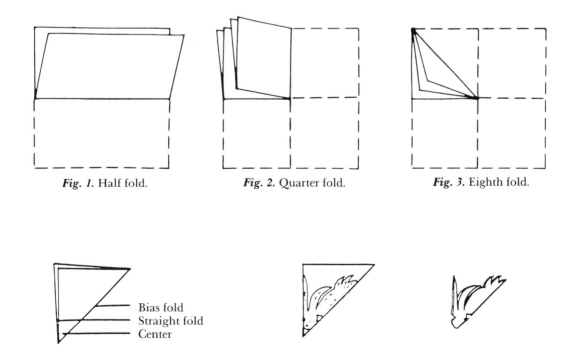

Fig. 1. Half fold.   *Fig. 2.* Quarter fold.   *Fig. 3.* Eighth fold.

Bias fold
Straight fold
Center

Fig. 4.   *Fig. 5.* Pin pattern to folded square.   *Fig. 6.* Cut out design.

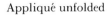

Appliqué unfolded

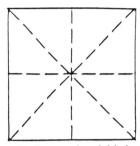

Background unfolded

Fig. 7.

background (*Fig. 7*). Place the appliqué design, right side up, on the background, matching the fold lines; this will automatically center the design. Starting in the center and working out, pin the design to the background. Baste along the fold lines with large stitches (*Fig. 8*); remove the pins. Starting from the center, baste around the design, ½″ in from the edge (*Fig. 9*); ease potential puckers as you baste.

Fig. 8. Match up fold lines; pin, then baste along folds.

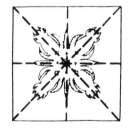

Fig. 9. Baste around design, ½″ from edge.

APPLIQUÉING THE DESIGN

In Hawaiian quilting, you do not turn under and baste the edge of the design before attaching it to the background fabric. Instead, turn under about ⅛″ to ¼″ on the edge of the fabric, just ahead of the stitching, using the edge of the needle to help turn the fabric under. Attach the design to the background with a blind stitch or a whipstitch, having at least 8 to 12 stitches to the inch. The stitches should be almost invisible.

To make a point (Figs. 10–12). Turn the working edge under. Appliqué to within ½″ of the point. Turn under the point, then turn under the other edge. Finish appliquéing the point. Be sure to take a stitch at the very tip to hold it securely in place.

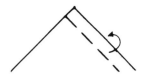

Fig. 10. Turn under first edge; appliqué to within ½″ of point.

Fig. 11. Turn under point.

Fig. 12. Turn under and appliqué remaining edge.

To make a reverse point (Fig. 13). Turn under the fabric edge to the bottom of the "V" on one side. The turn-under allowance will decrease to practically nothing at the bottom. Appliqué the straight edge to the "V," take several stitches at the "V" to prevent fraying, then reverse the process to appliqué the remaining straight edge.

Fig. 13. Reverse point.

To make an outside curve (Fig. 14). Following the curve of the design, turn under the edge and appliqué.

Fig. 14. Outside curve.

To make an inside curve (Fig. 15). Following the curve of the design, turn the edge under and appliqué. You should not have to snip the fabric in the curve, merely ease under less fabric where necessary and secure with extra stitches.

Fig. 15. Inside curve.

After the design is appliquéd, remove the basting stitches. Using a damp press cloth, press the block, pressing out the fold creases. *This will be your last chance to press the block.*

ASSEMBLY

Each design in this book includes a diagram of suggested quilting lines, or you can create your own. You can mark the quilting lines on the fabric with a water-erasable pen, although you may not find this necessary, since the quilting should follow the outline of the appliquéd design. Be sure to test any marking tools on a scrap of fabric before using them on your quilt block.

Place the backing square, wrong side up, on the table; place the batting square on top of it. Place the appliquéd square, right side up, on top of the batting (*Fig. 16*). Starting in the center and working toward the edges, pin the three layers together, smoothing out puckers. Again starting in the center and working toward the edges, baste the layers together in horizontal and vertical lines about 3″ apart (*Fig 17*). Remove the pins. Place the block in a large hoop if desired.

Fig. 16. Pin appliqué, batting and muslin squares together.

Fig. 17. Baste together with a 3″ grid pattern; remove pins.

QUILTING

Quilting is *not* done with a running stitch, but rather with an up-and-down motion, so that the needle enters the fabric at a right angle. It is because of this angle that the contour of the quilting is so pronounced.

Use a single length of thread not more than 20″ long for quilting. Put one to three knots in the end of the thread. Insert the needle through the backing and run the needle through the batting at an angle. Pull the needle through the top fabric until the tension of the knot is felt. Gently, but firmly, pull the knot through the backing into the batting. Take a backstitch to secure the thread, then begin quilting. To end the thread, take

a backstitch and run the needle through the batting. Bring the needle out through the backing, pull the thread taut and cut it very close to the surface of the fabric. The thread end should vanish into the batting.

The first row of quilting is worked on the background exactly next to the appliquéd edge. Subsequent rows of quilting should be placed a uniform distance apart—½″ to 1″.

When the quilting has been completed, take out all basting.

FINISHING

Binding a single block. From the fabric used for the appliqué, cut binding strips 1½″ wide; join to make a strip long enough to go around the square, plus 2″ to 3″.

Turn in ¼″ at the end of the strip. Right sides together, matching raw edges, pin the strip around the block, mitering the corners. Lap the raw end over the folded end; cut off the excess. Stitch around ¼″ from the edges. Fold the binding over the edges of the block to the back; turn in the raw edge. Slip-stitch the folded edge and the mitered corners in place.

Making a pillow. Press the pillow back; do not press the quilted block. Pin the block to the pillow back with the right sides together. The quilting will make the appliquéd block draw up slightly, so you will probably have to trim the pillow back to fit. Stitch ¼″ from the edge of the fabric around three sides and four corners (*Fig. 18*). Trim the corners and turn the piece right side out. Insert the pillow form; turn in and pin the unstitched edge. Blind-stitch in place. Remove the pins.

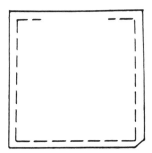

Fig. 18. Stitch around three sides and four corners.

Joining blocks. The blocks can be joined to form larger projects such as wall hangings or bed covers. They can, of course, be arranged and sewn together before they are quilted; however, they lend themselves to the "quilt-as-you-go" method of assembly.

For this method, quilt each block as described above, but be sure to end all quilting at least ½″ from the edges. Trim the batting ¼″ smaller than the top; fold the backing out of the way. Right sides in, pin the blocks together, pinning through the appliquéd front only. Stitch ¼″ from the edge. Lap the backing of one block over the backing of the other, turn under the raw edge and slip-stitch in place. Bind the edges of the completed piece or turn in the raw edges and slip-stitch them together.

METRIC CONVERSION CHART

CONVERTING INCHES TO CENTIMETERS AND YARDS TO METERS

mm — millimeters   cm — centimeters   m — meters

INCHES INTO MILLIMETERS AND CENTIMETERS
(Slightly rounded off for convenience)

inches	mm		cm	inches	cm	inches	cm	inches	cm
⅛	3mm			5	12.5	21	53.5	38	96.5
¼	6mm			5½	14	22	56	39	99
⅜	10mm	or	1cm	6	15	23	58.5	40	101.5
½	13mm	or	1.3cm	7	18	24	61	41	104
⅝	15mm	or	1.5cm	8	20.5	25	63.5	42	106.5
¾	20mm	or	2cm	9	23	26	66	43	109
⅞	22mm	or	2.2cm	10	25.5	27	68.5	44	112
1	25mm	or	2.5cm	11	28	28	71	45	114.5
1¼	32mm	or	3.2cm	12	30.5	29	73.5	46	117
1½	38mm	or	3.8cm	13	33	30	76	47	119.5
1¾	45mm	or	4.5cm	14	35.5	31	79	48	122
2	50mm	or	5cm	15	38	32	81.5	49	124.5
2½	65mm	or	6.5cm	16	40.5	33	84	50	127
3	75mm	or	7.5cm	17	43	34	86.5		
3½	90mm	or	9cm	18	46	35	89		
4	100mm	or	10cm	19	48.5	36	91.5		
4½	115mm	or	11.5cm	20	51	37	94		

• YARDS TO METERS
(Slightly rounded off for convenience)

yards	meters	yards	meters	yards	meters	yards	meters	yards	meters
⅛	0.15	2⅛	1.95	4⅛	3.80	6⅛	5.60	8⅛	7.45
¼	0.25	2¼	2.10	4¼	3.90	6¼	5.75	8¼	7.55
⅜	0.35	2⅜	2.20	4⅜	4.00	6⅜	5.85	8⅜	7.70
½	0.50	2½	2.30	4½	4.15	6½	5.95	8½	7.80
⅝	0.60	2⅝	2.40	4⅝	4.25	6⅝	6.10	8⅝	7.90
¾	0.70	2¾	2.55	4¾	4.35	6¾	6.20	8¾	8.00
⅞	0.80	2⅞	2.65	4⅞	4.50	6⅞	6.30	8⅞	8.15
1	0.95	3	2.75	5	4.60	7	6.40	9	8.25
1⅛	1.05	3⅛	2.90	5⅛	4.70	7⅛	6.55	9⅛	8.35
1¼	1.15	3¼	3.00	5¼	4.80	7¼	6.65	9¼	8.50
1⅜	1.30	3⅜	3.10	5⅜	4.95	7⅜	6.75	9⅜	8.60
1½	1.40	3½	3.20	5½	5.05	7½	6.90	9½	8.70
1⅝	1.50	3⅝	3.35	5⅝	5.15	7⅝	7.00	9⅝	8.80
1¾	1.60	3¾	3.45	5¾	5.30	7¾	7.10	9¾	8.95
1⅞	1.75	3⅞	3.55	5⅞	5.40	7⅞	7.20	9⅞	9.05
2	1.85	4	3.70	6	5.50	8	7.35	10	9.15

AVAILABLE FABRIC WIDTHS

25"	65cm	50"	127cm
27"	70cm	54"/56"	140cm
35"/36"	90cm	58"/60"	150cm
39"	100cm	68"/70"	175cm
44"/45"	115cm	72"	180cm
48"	122cm		

AVAILABLE ZIPPER LENGTHS

4"	10cm	10"	25cm	22"	55cm
5"	12cm	12"	30cm	24"	60cm
6"	15cm	14"	35cm	26"	65cm
7"	18cm	16"	40cm	28"	70cm
8"	20cm	18"	45cm	30"	75cm
9"	22cm	20"	50cm		

Angel's Trumpet

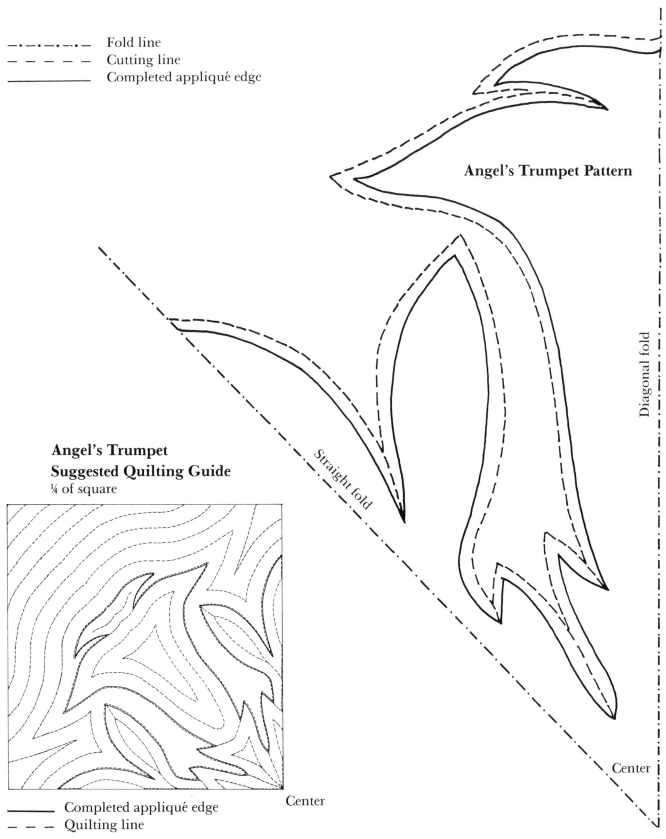

-··-··-··- Fold line

- - - - Cutting line

———— Completed appliqué edge

Angel's Trumpet Pattern

Diagonal fold

Straight fold

Center

**Angel's Trumpet
Suggested Quilting Guide**
¼ of square

Center

———— Completed appliqué edge

- - - Quilting line

Anthurium

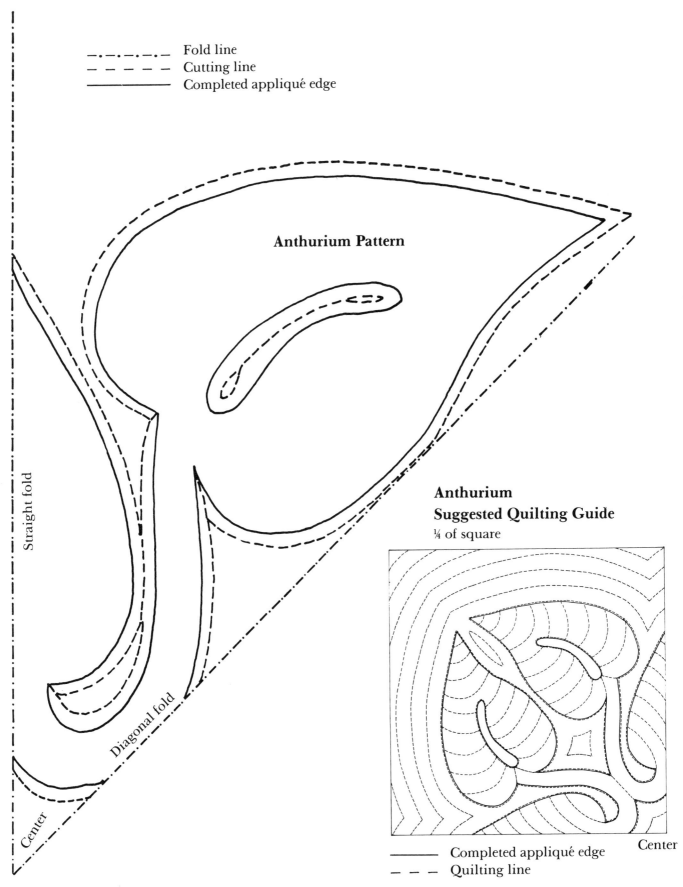

Fold line
Cutting line
Completed appliqué edge

Anthurium Pattern

Straight fold

Diagonal fold

Center

**Anthurium
Suggested Quilting Guide**
¼ of square

Completed appliqué edge
Quilting line

Center

Blue Jade

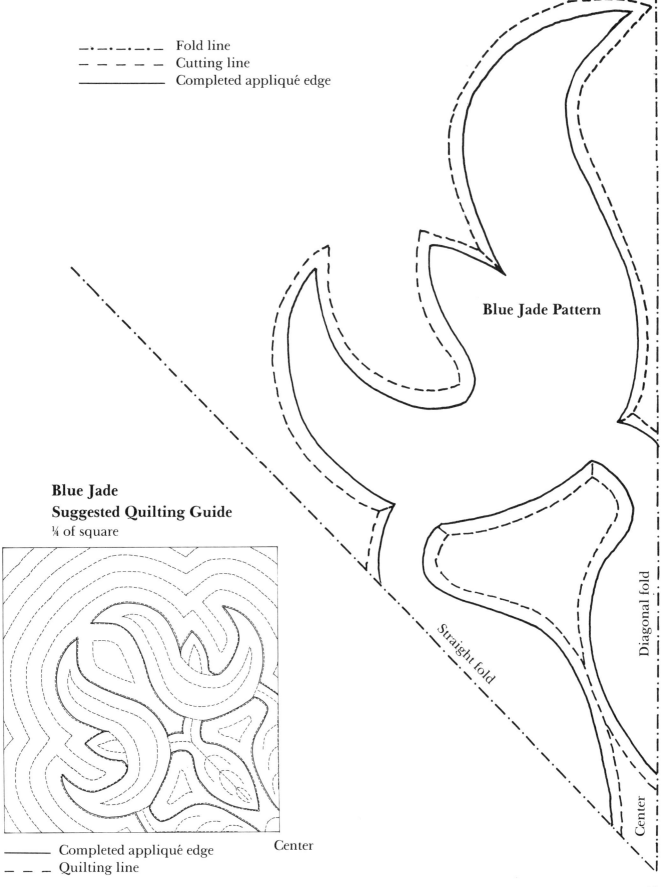

Fold line
Cutting line
Completed appliqué edge

Blue Jade Pattern

Blue Jade
Suggested Quilting Guide
¼ of square

Completed appliqué edge
Quilting line

Center

Straight fold

Diagonal fold

Center

Breadfruit

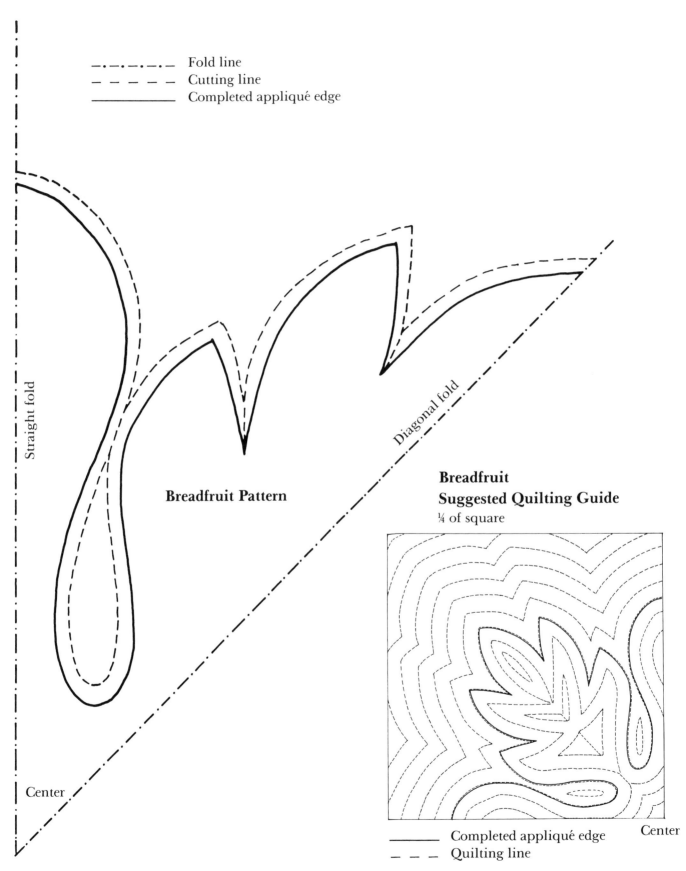

Fold line
Cutting line
Completed appliqué edge

Straight fold

Center

Diagonal fold

Breadfruit Pattern

**Breadfruit
Suggested Quilting Guide**
¼ of square

Center

Completed appliqué edge
Quilting line

Calla Lily

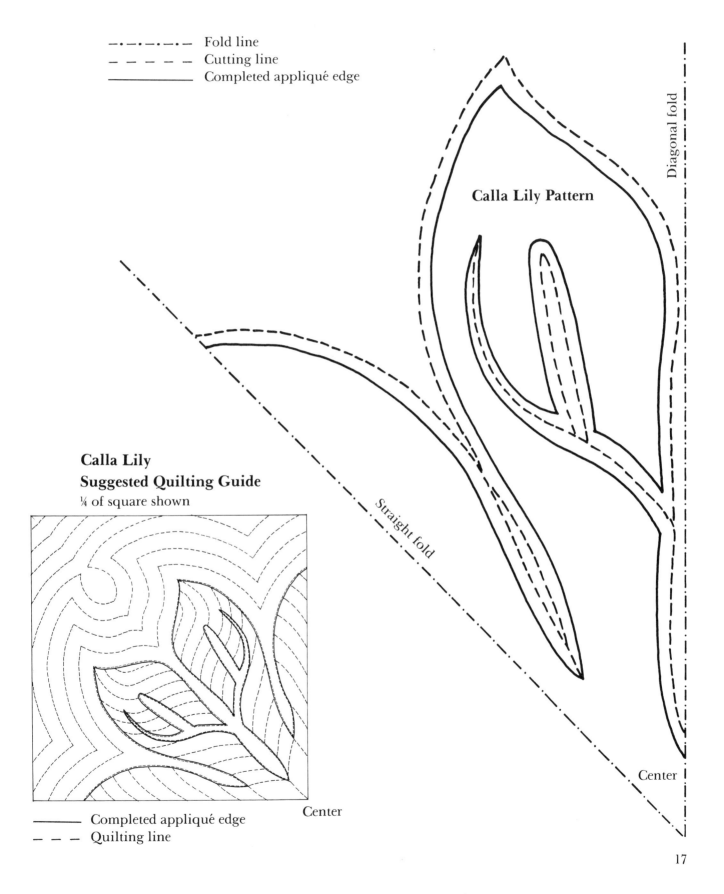

Fold line
Cutting line
Completed appliqué edge

Diagonal fold

Calla Lily Pattern

Straight fold

Calla Lily
Suggested Quilting Guide
¼ of square shown

Completed appliqué edge
Quilting line

Center

Center

Crown Flower

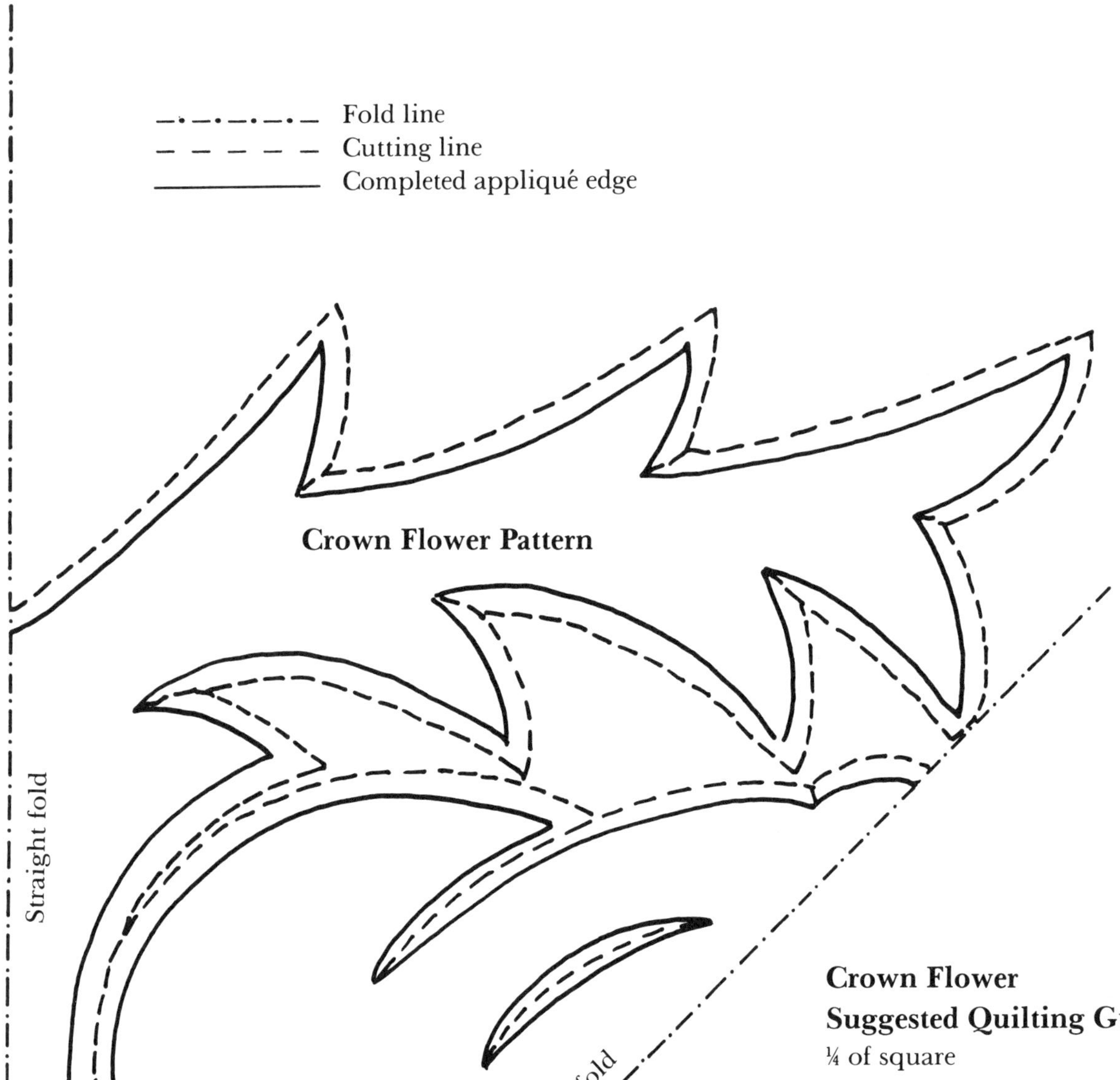

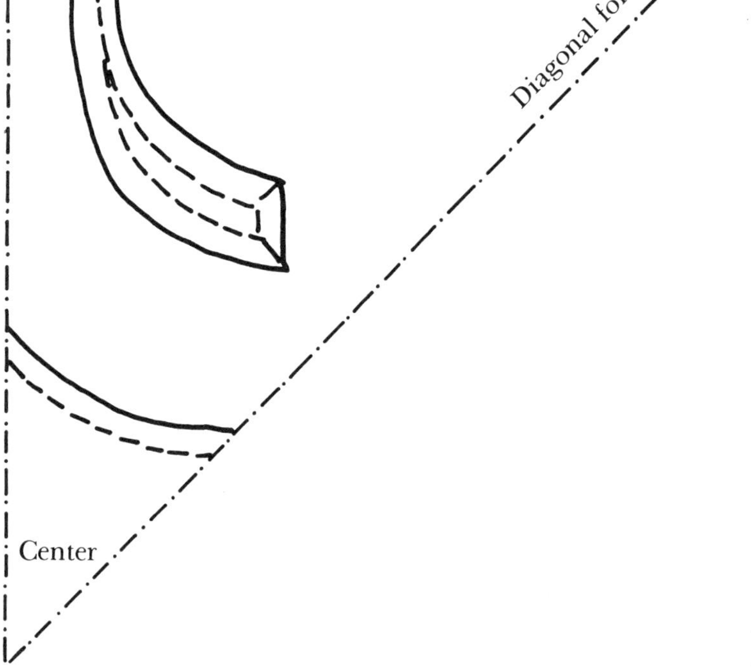

_ . _ . _ . _ . _   Fold line
_ _ _ _ _ _ _   Cutting line
_____   Completed appliqué edge

Crown Flower Pattern

Straight fold

Diagonal fold

Center

**Crown Flower
Suggested Quilting Guide**
¼ of square

Center

_____   Completed appliqué edge
_ _ _ _ _ _   Quilting line

Hibiscus

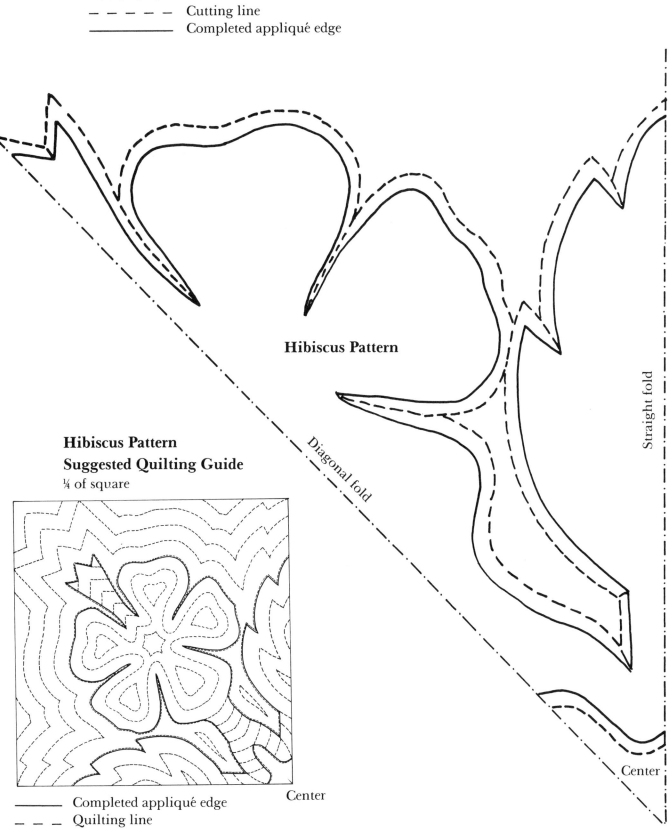

_.._.._.. — Fold line
_ _ _ _ — Cutting line
——— Completed appliqué edge

Hibiscus Pattern

Straight fold

Diagonal fold

Hibiscus Pattern
Suggested Quilting Guide
¼ of square

——— Completed appliqué edge
_ _ _ Quilting line

Center

Center

Hoya

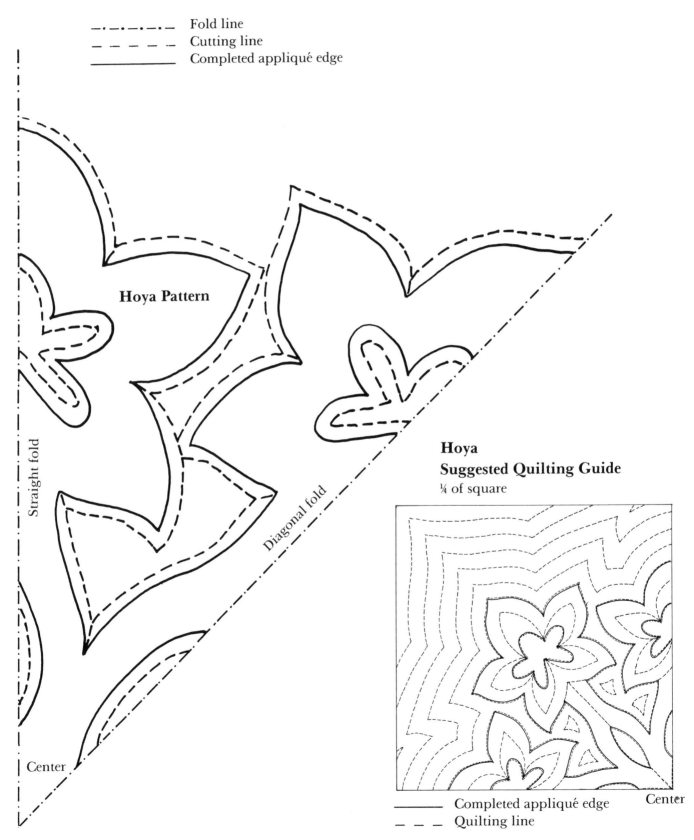

Fold line
Cutting line
Completed appliqué edge

Hoya Pattern

Straight fold

Diagonal fold

Center

Hoya
Suggested Quilting Guide
¼ of square

Completed appliqué edge
Quilting line

Center

24

Iris

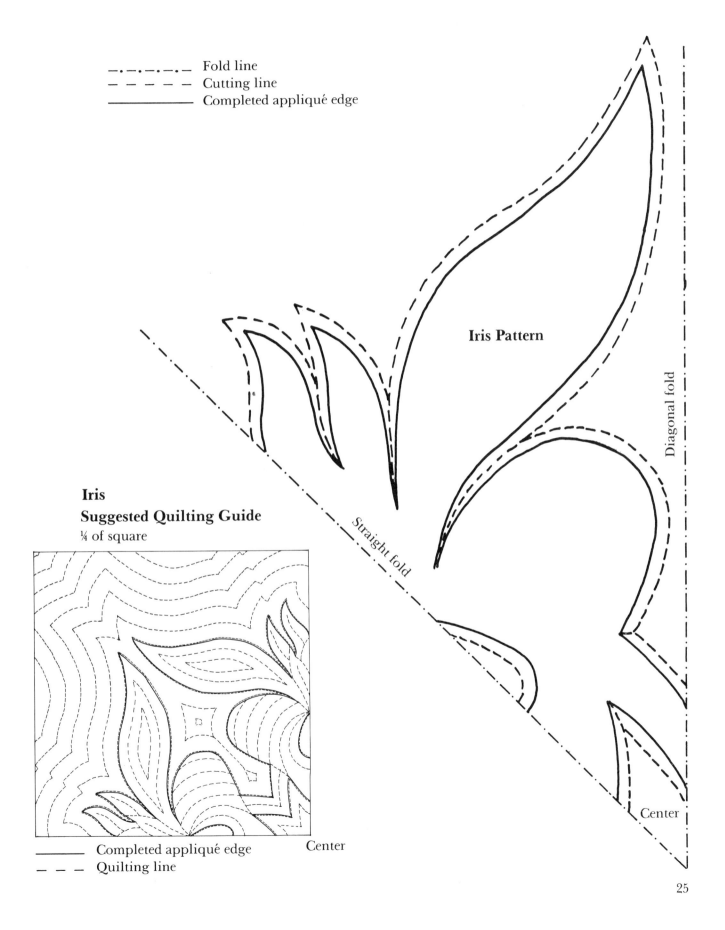

—·—·—·—·— Fold line

— — — — Cutting line

————— Completed appliqué edge

Iris Pattern

Diagonal fold

Straight fold

Iris
Suggested Quilting Guide
¼ of square

————— Completed appliqué edge

— — — Quilting line

Center

Center

Kukui

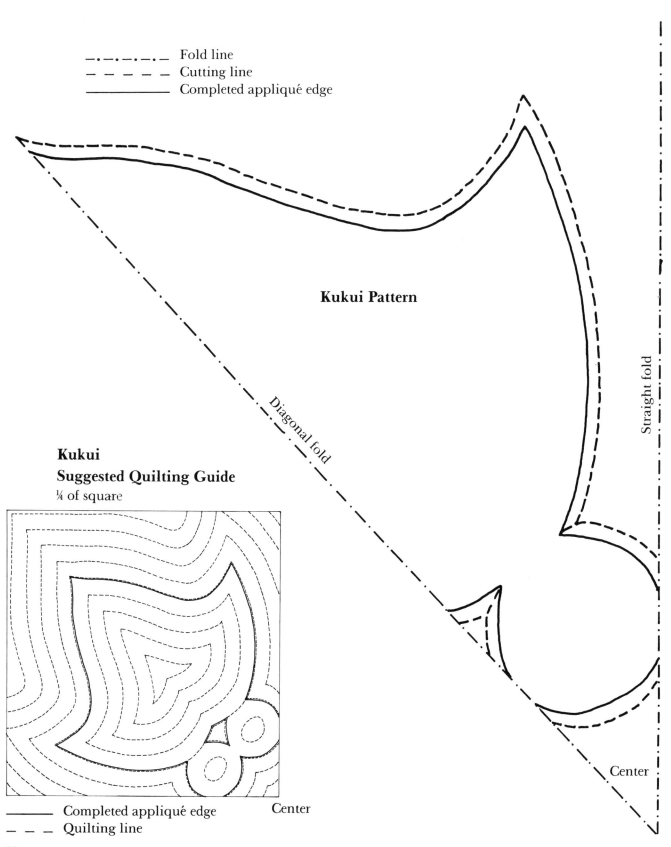

Fold line
Cutting line
Completed appliqué edge

Kukui Pattern

Diagonal fold

Straight fold

Kukui
Suggested Quilting Guide
¼ of square

Completed appliqué edge
Quilting line

Center

Center

Maile

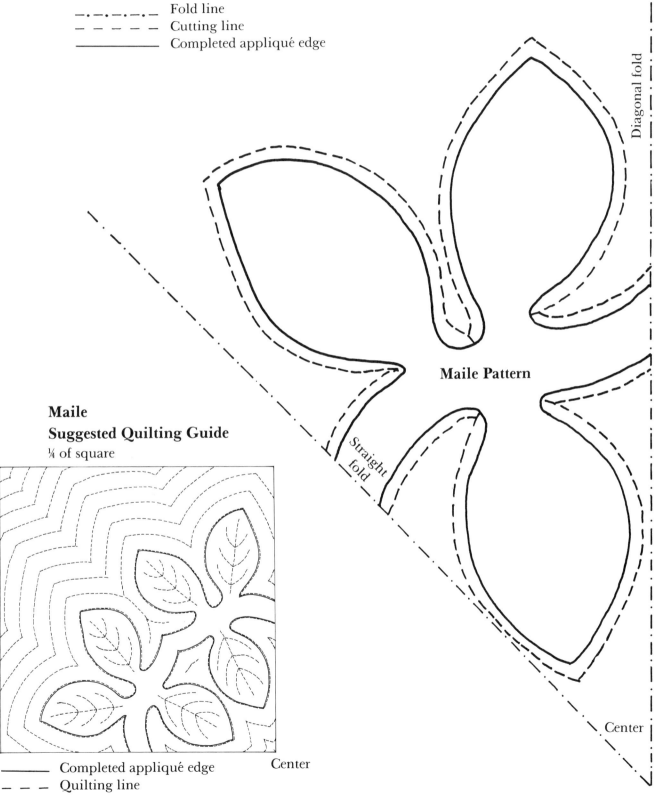

Fold line —.—.—.—.—
Cutting line — — — — —
Completed appliqué edge ————

Maile Pattern

Diagonal fold

Straight fold

Center

Maile
Suggested Quilting Guide
¼ of square

———— Completed appliqué edge
— — — Quilting line

Center

Orchid

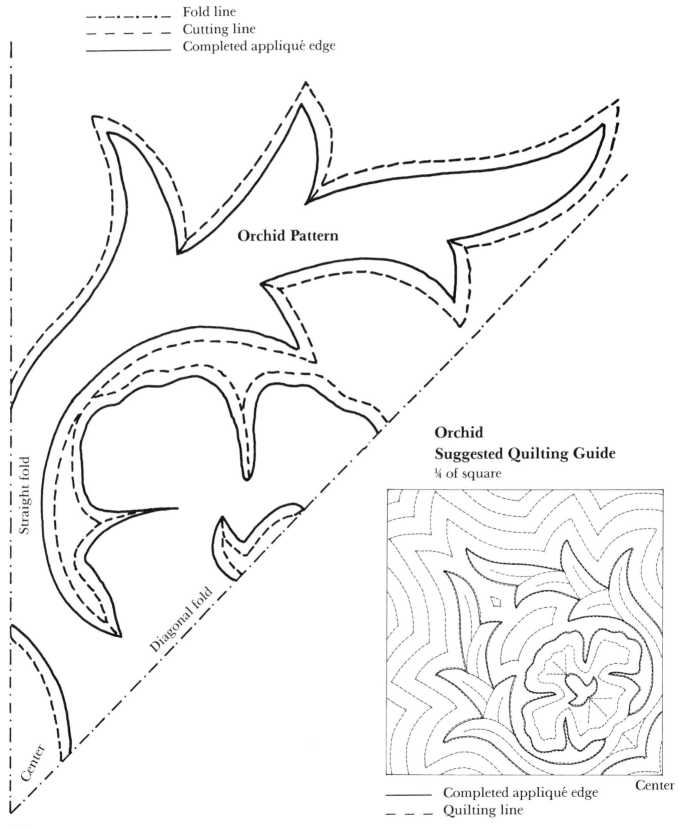

Fold line
Cutting line
Completed appliqué edge

Orchid Pattern

Straight fold

Diagonal fold

Center

Orchid
Suggested Quilting Guide
¼ of square

Completed appliqué edge
Quilting line

Center

Pineapple

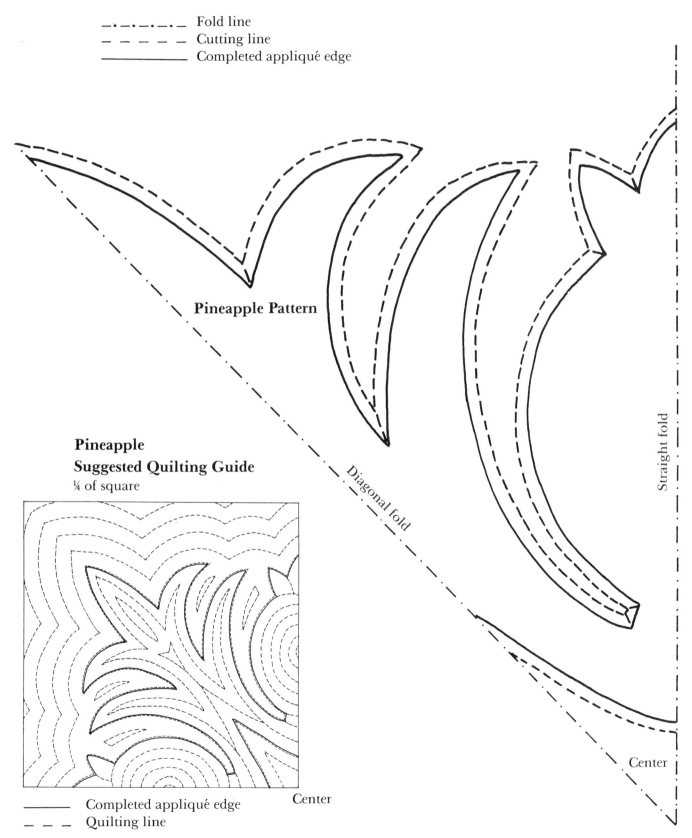

Fold line —.—.—.—.—
Cutting line — — — — —
Completed appliqué edge ————

Pineapple Pattern

Pineapple
Suggested Quilting Guide
¼ of square

Diagonal fold

Straight fold

Center

Center

———— Completed appliqué edge
— — — Quilting line

Plumeria

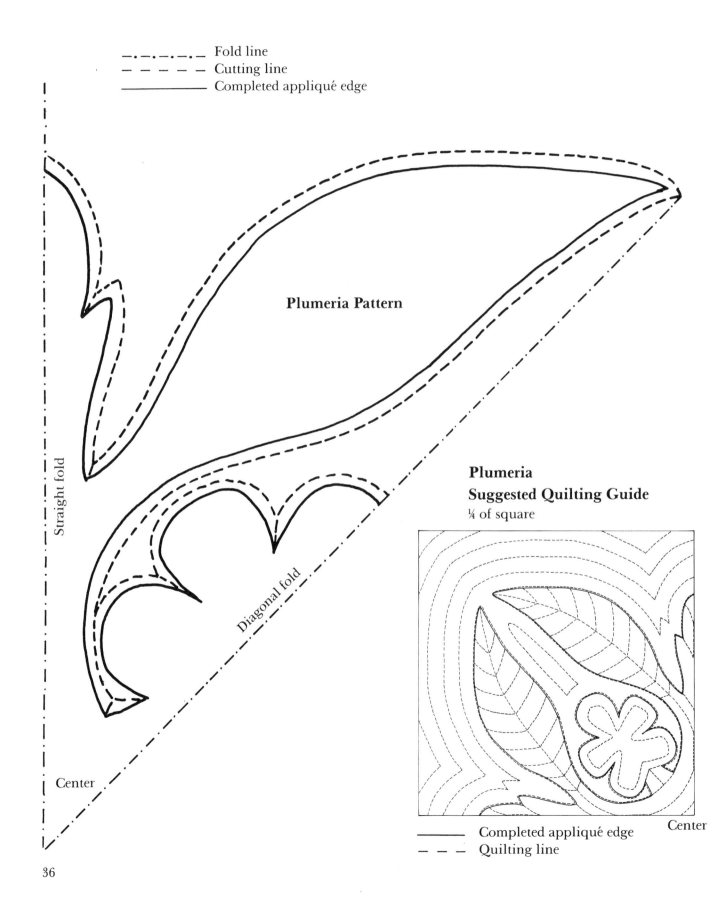

- — · — · — · — Fold line
- — — — — — Cutting line
- ———————— Completed appliqué edge

Plumeria Pattern

Straight fold

Diagonal fold

Center

**Plumeria
Suggested Quilting Guide**
¼ of square

Center

- ———————— Completed appliqué edge
- — — — — Quilting line

Protea

Fold line
Cutting line
Completed appliqué edge

Protea Pattern
Diagonal fold
Straight fold
Center

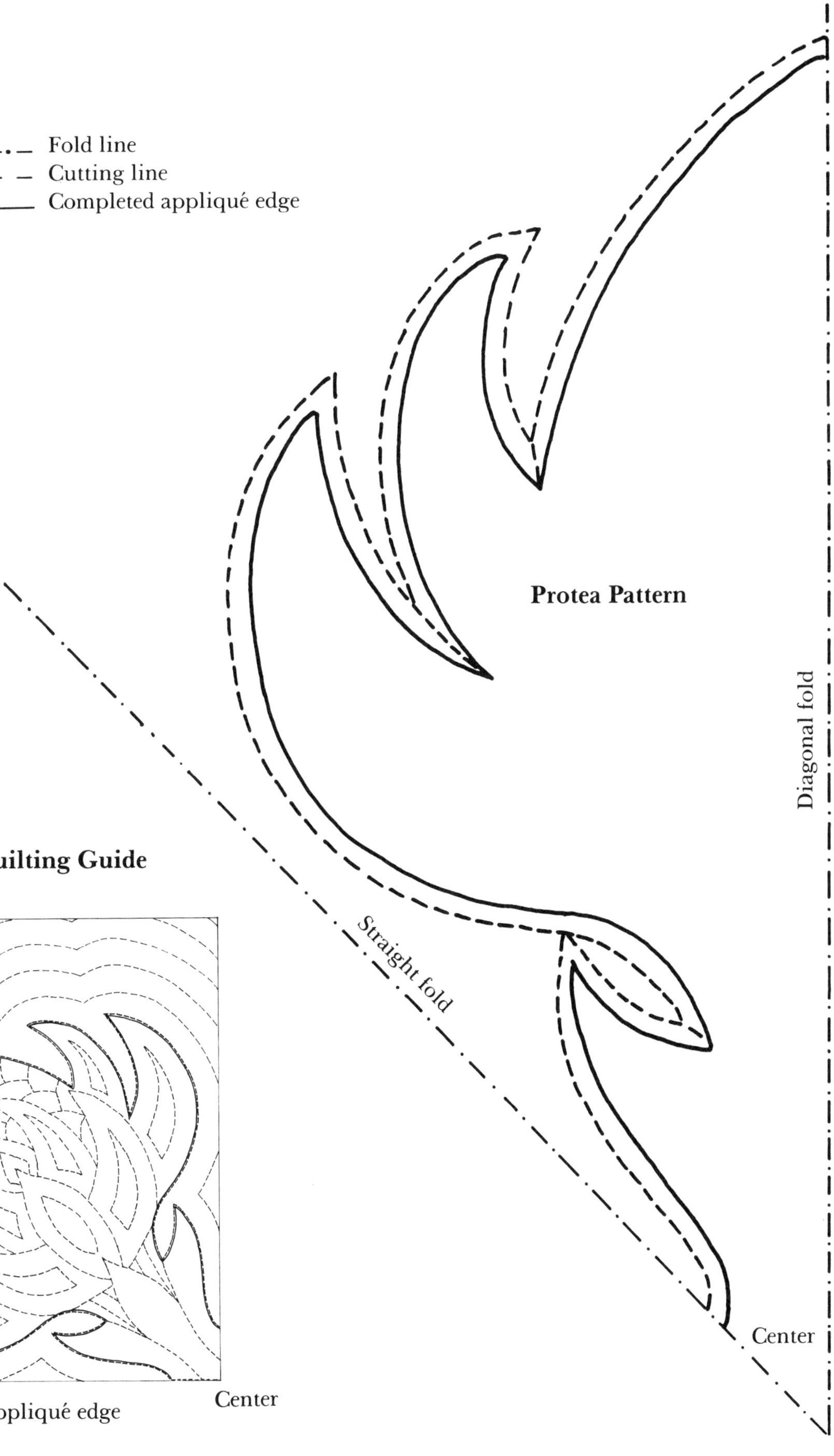

Protea
Suggested Quilting Guide
¼ of square

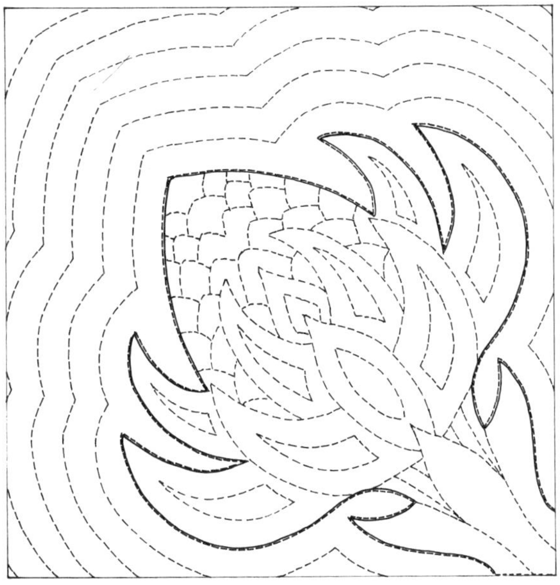

Center

Completed appliqué edge
Quilting line

Red Ginger

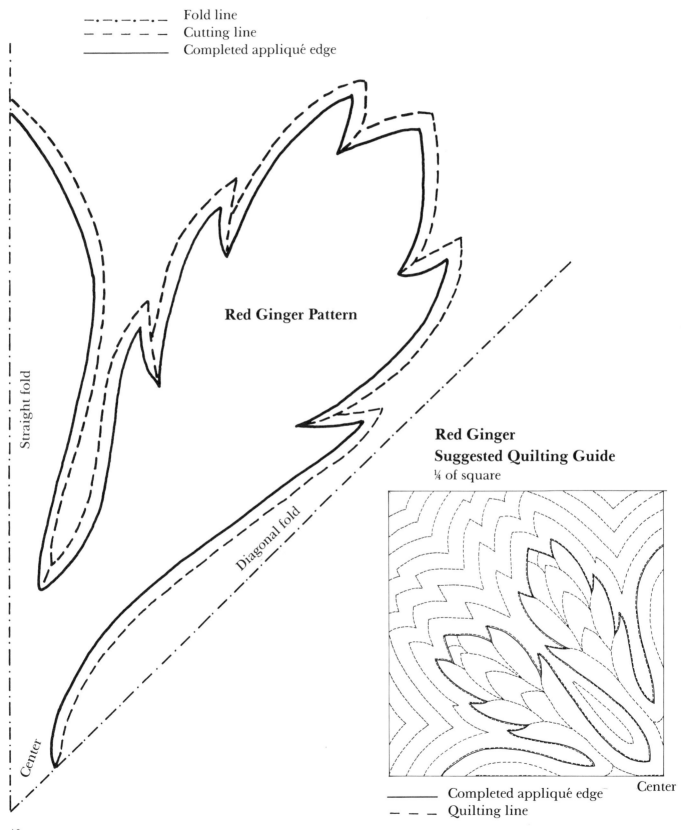

Fold line
Cutting line
Completed appliqué edge

Straight fold

Red Ginger Pattern

Diagonal fold

Center

**Red Ginger
Suggested Quilting Guide**
¼ of square

Center

Completed appliqué edge
Quilting line

Trumpet Vine

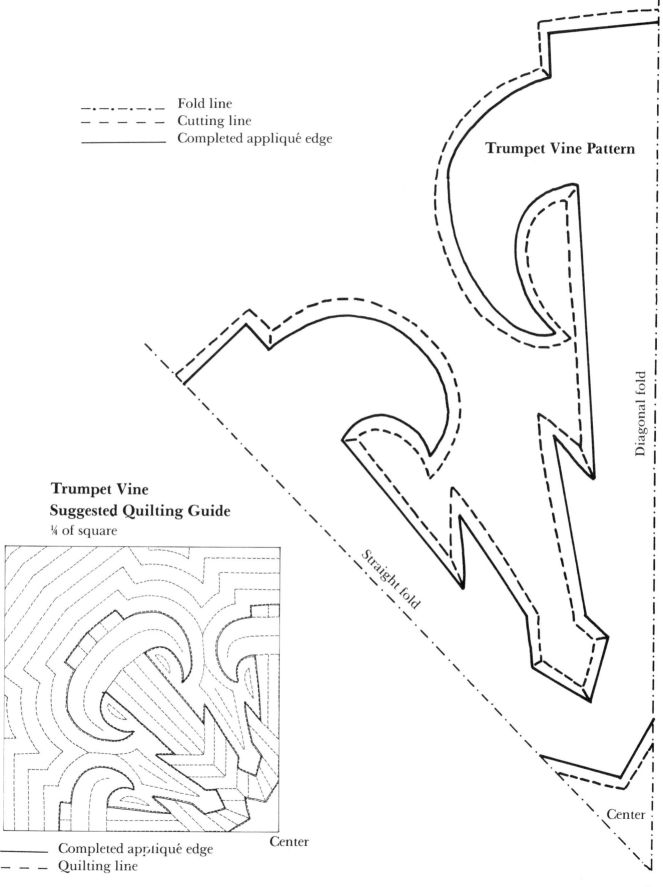

—·—·—·—	Fold line
——————	Cutting line
——————————	Completed appliqué edge

Trumpet Vine Pattern

Diagonal fold

Straight fold

**Trumpet Vine
Suggested Quilting Guide**

¼ of square

Center

—————— Completed appliqué edge

— — — Quilting line

Center

Tuberose

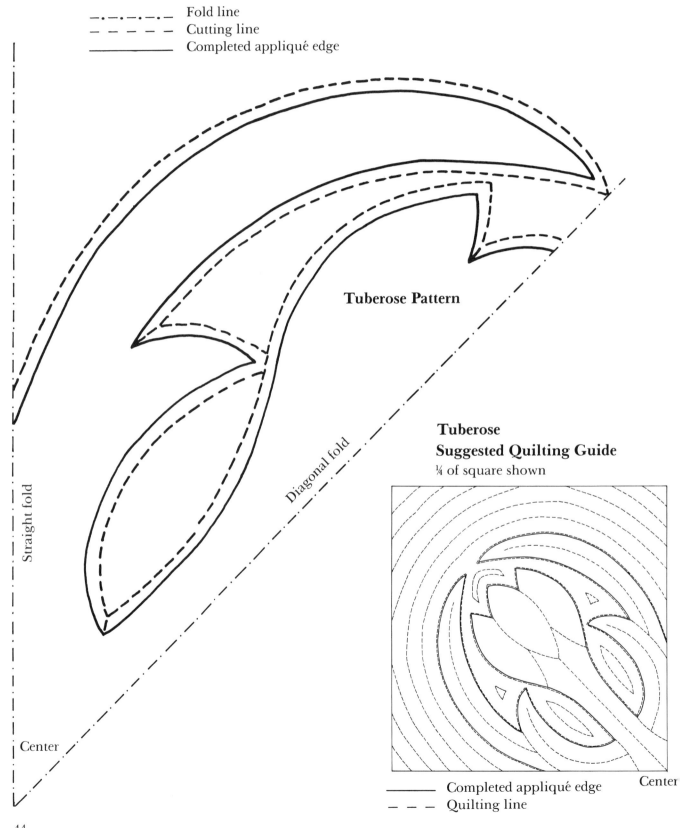

Fold line
Cutting line
Completed appliqué edge

Straight fold

Diagonal fold

Center

Tuberose Pattern

Tuberose
Suggested Quilting Guide
¼ of square shown

Center

Completed appliqué edge
Quilting line

Water Lily

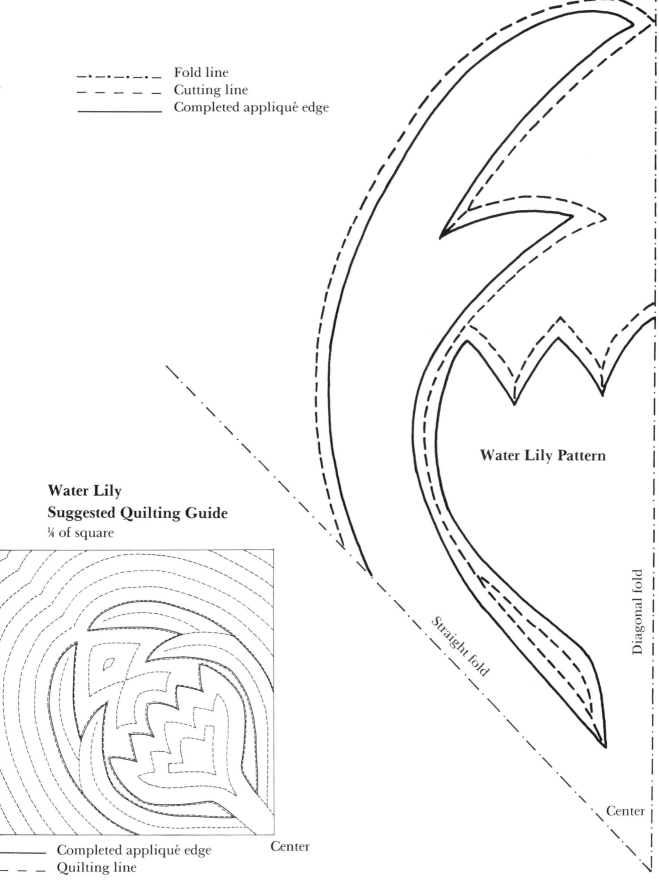

Fold line ·—·—·—·—·
Cutting line — — — — —
Completed appliqué edge ————

Water Lily Pattern

Diagonal fold

Straight fold

Center

Water Lily
Suggested Quilting Guide
¼ of square

———— Completed appliqué edge
— — — Quilting line

Center

Wood Rose

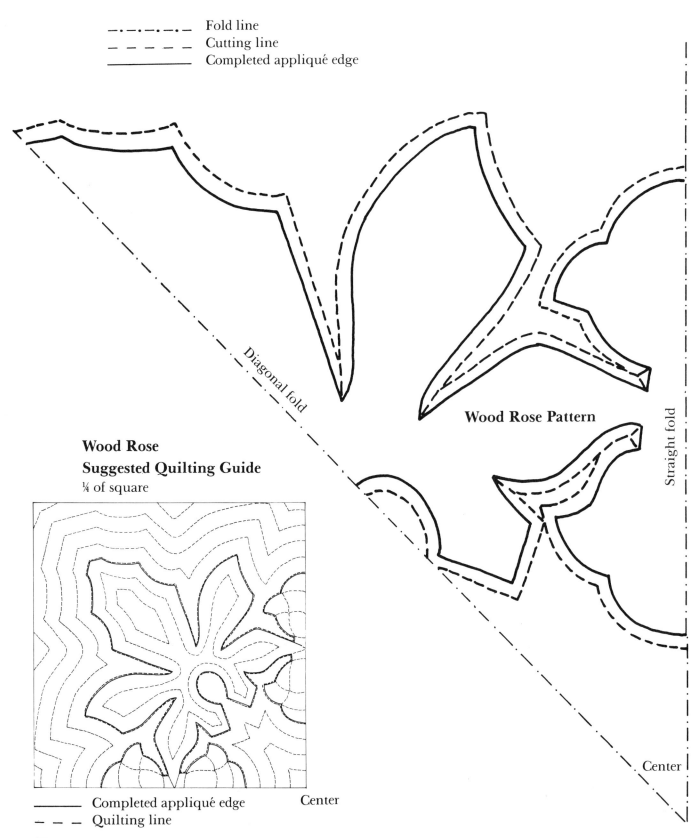

- —·—·—·— Fold line
- — — — — Cutting line
- ————— Completed appliqué edge

Diagonal fold

Wood Rose Pattern

Straight fold

Wood Rose
Suggested Quilting Guide
¼ of square

Center

Center

- ————— Completed appliqué edge
- — — — Quilting line